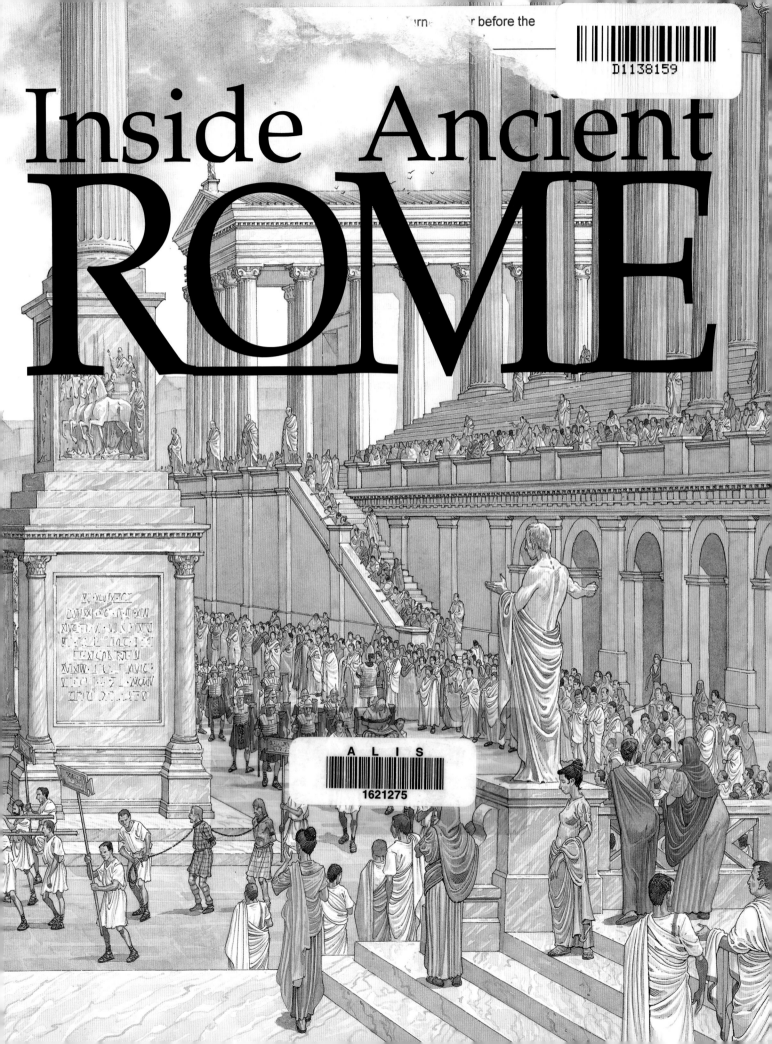

Inside Ancient
ROME

Author: David Stewart has written many non-fiction books for children.
He lives in Brighton with his wife and son.

Artists:

David Antram was born in Brighton, England, in 1958. He studied at Eastbourne College of
Art and has illustrated many children's non-fiction books.

Mark Bergin was born in Hastings, England, in 1961. He studied at Eastbourne College of
Art and has specialised in historical reconstructions, aviation and maritime subjects since 1983.

John James was born in London in 1959. He studied at Eastbourne College of Art and has
specialised in historical reconstruction since leaving art school in 1982.

Fact Consultant: Dr Stephen Johnson, Director of Operations, Heritage Lottery Fund, and
author of several books on Roman Archaeology.

Editors: Sophie Izod and Carolyn Franklin

DTP Designer: Mark Williams

Published in Great Britain in 2005 by
Book House, an imprint of
The Salariya Book Company Ltd
25 Marlborough Place, Brighton BN1 1UB

Please visit The Salariya Book Company at: **www.salariya.com**

ISBN 1 904642 98-5

Visit our website at **www.book-house.co.uk** for free electronic versions of:
You Wouldn't Want To Be an Egyptian Mummy!
You Wouldn't Want To Be a Roman Gladiator!
Avoid joining Shackleton's Polar Expedition!
Avoid sailing on a 19th-century Whaling Ship!
Due to the changing nature of internet links, The Salariya Book Company has developed
an online list of websites related to the subject of this book. This site is updated regularly.
Please use this link to access the list: **http://www.salariya.com/inside/rome**

A catalogue record for this book is available from the British Library.
Printed and bound in China.
Manufactured by Leo Paper Products Ltd.

Photographic credits

Ancient Art & Architecture Collection Ltd: 38
The Art Archive / Archaeological Museum Milan /
Dagli Orti: 34
The Art Archive / Archaeological Museum Naples /
Dagli Orti: 30, 32
The Art Archive / Archaeological Museum Timgad
Algeria / Dagli Orti: 25
The Art Archive / Dagli Orti: 15
The Art Archive / Dagli Orti (A): 37

The Art Archive / Musée du Louvre Paris / Dagli
Orti: 9
The Art Archive / Museo della Civilta Romana Rome
/ Dagli Orti (A): 26, 39, 41
The Art Archive / Siritide Museum Policoro / Dagli
Orti (A): 33

Every effort has been made to trace copyright holders.
The Salariya Book Company apologises for any
unintentional omissions and would be pleased, in such
cases, to add an acknowledgment in future editions.

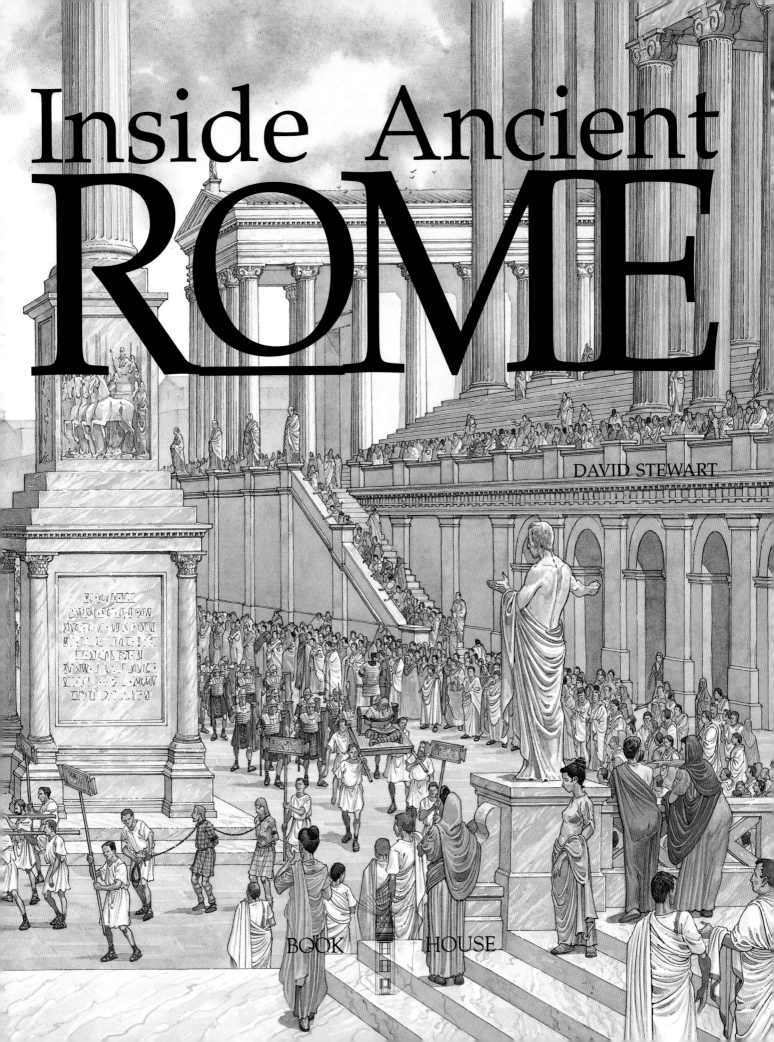

Inside Ancient ROME

DAVID STEWART

BOOK HOUSE

CONTENTS

INTRODUCTION

Rome was the largest and most famous city in the ancient world; its magnificent public buildings symbolising the wealth of the Roman Empire. By the time of the Emperor Augustus (c.31 BC) it had a population of over a million people. Rome's history can be divided into three periods: the rule of Kings (c.753-509 BC), the Republic (c.509-31 BC) and the Roman Empire ruled over by emperors (c.31 BC-AD 476). By the time Roman power collapsed in the fifth century AD, Rome had succeeded in uniting many people and lands under one government.

Our knowledge of Ancient Rome comes from a variety of sources: the Roman buildings and structures that are still in existence; the writings that have been passed down; and artefacts that have been unearthed by excavations. The Romans based many of their ideas for architecture, religion, literature, art and politics on those of the Ancient Greeks.

The influence of Ancient Roman civilisation was so powerful that it is still with us today. For example, many European languages, including English, use Latin words or words that have Latin roots. Similarly, when Christianity became the official religion of Rome, the Catholic Church adopted Roman ideas and traditions and spread them throughout the Empire. As a result, The Twelve Tables and the written law of the Emperor Justinian (The Justinian Code) still form the basis of western law.

This book explores Rome, the city at the centre of the vast Roman Empire.

THE ROMAN EMPIRE

Rome dominated the known world for almost a thousand years. However, this time was spent in almost constant warfare with its 'barbarian' neighbours. The Empire reached its peak under the Emperor Trajan (AD 98 -117), with its borders stretching from Scotland to the Black Sea in modern Turkey. From west to east it extended for 4300 km and from north to south for 3200 km, and some 50 million people lived within its borders. The spoils of war made Rome rich. People, slaves and luxury goods poured into Rome from all over the Empire. But, from the end of the 2nd century AD, the Empire came increasingly under threat from outside forces who wanted a share of its wealth. Rome went into a slow but steady decline. After the city's fall in AD 476 the centre of the Empire moved to Constantinople (present day Istanbul), where it continued until around 1453.

The provinces, those lands conquered by the Romans, formed the major part of the Empire. Roman citizens had certain rights and duties that did not apply to non-citizens. Only citizens could vote, work in government, or attend the public games - but they also had to pay taxes for these privileges. The Emperor Caracalla (211-217 BC) extended citizenship to all provincials, a cunning move, as this allowed him to collect taxes from many more people.

The map (right) shows the Roman Empire at its greatest size, under the Emperor Trajan. Trajan's successor, Hadrian, thought the Empire was getting too large to control. He stopped its expansion and tried to consolidate and fortify existing Roman lands.

People of the Roman Empire

a   b   c   d

e   f   g   h

The Roman Empire was made up of many different peoples **a**. a Dacian from what is now modern Romania; **b**. Celtic-speakers from Gaul (France) or Britain; **c**. a Numidian from North Africa; **d**. a Roman citizen; **e**. a Greek; **f**. a Syrian woman; **g**. a Jewish priest from Judaea; **h**. a Palmyrene woman from Jordan.

The globe (below) shows how far the Roman Empire extended.

Celtic farmer

Aqueduct

HISPANIA

Cordoba

Northern horsemen

Attacking the Empire's frontiers

GERMANIA

ondinium

Grain

Defending the Empire's frontiers

Prisoners of war

Skins

GAUL

Military fort

Ravenna

DACIA

Amphora

BLACK   SEA

ITALY

Senator

Marseilles

Rome

Pergamum

Bridge

ragona

Naples

GREECE

Smyrna

MEDITERRANEAN SEA

Athens

Ephesus

Damascus

Corinth

Antioch

Carthage

SICILY

CRETE

CYPRUS

Temple

Trading ship

Jerusalem

AFRICA

Lepcis Magna

Cyrene

Alexandria

Market building

Pyramids

EGYPT

Roman colonist

FROM VILLAGE TO EMPIRE

The city of Rome grew from a small group of peasant settlements built on the seven hills of Rome at a point where the River Tiber could easily be crossed. Before the Romans Italy was occupied by a variety of tribes: Greeks, Etruscans, Samnites, Latins, Sabines, and Umbrians all settled there, living in simple huts and farming the fertile soil. From among this group of early farmers, it was the Latins who came to dominate the region and, in time, became known as the Romans. Some of the early Kings of Rome were Etruscan. In 509 BC Roman nobles drove out the seventh and last king, Tarquinius Superbus (Tarquin the Proud), and set up a republic. The Romans hated the title of 'king' thereafter. The government of the new republic was in the hands of the patricians, a group of Roman noblemen.

This famous statue shows the she-wolf suckling Romulus and Remus.

Legend has it that Rome was founded in 753 BC by twins called Romulus and Remus, the sons of Mars, the god of war and Rhea Silvia (King Numitor's daughter). When they were just infants, the boys' wicked uncle had ordered that they be drowned in the River Tiber, but fortunately they were saved by a female wolf, and raised as her own. The twins grew up to found the new city and, after killing his brother in a quarrel, Romulus became the first King of Rome; it is from him that the city takes its name. The Ancient Romans calculated their dates A.U.C, which stood for *ab urbe condita*, meaning 'from the founding of the city'.

Statue of the river god, Tiberinus, personifying the River Tiber. Found in 1512, it shows Romulus and Remus with the she-wolf.

THE REPUBLIC

When Rome became a republic after the rebellion against Tarquin the Proud, the power previously held by the king was shared between two men called 'consuls', who held office for one year. A citizens' assembly and the Senate (a council) helped the consuls to govern. Roman citizens were either rich and powerful 'patricians' or poor and powerless 'plebians'. Between 494 and 287 BC the plebians made several mass withdrawals from the city, only returning when their demands for a political voice had been met. As a result, the people were allowed to elect two 'tribunes' to act as their representatives, who could stop any rulings of the Senate by calling "Veto!" (I forbid). These two groups were represented in the initials 'SPQR' - Senatus Populusque Romanus - the Senate and People of Rome, which became the symbol of Roman power.

SPQR (above) This proud symbol of the Roman state was carried by the army on its standards.

Coin of Nero Augustus (AD 54-68) called a *dupondius* (right), minted in Rome.

A POLITICAL CAREER

Only boys from wealthy families had a good education, studying Latin, Greek, philosophy, and rhetoric - the art of public speaking.

The army provided a good first step for rich and ambitious men who wanted to follow a career in politics.

The first government post was that of *quaestor*, a junior senator, who was in charge of finance and administration.

A successful quaestor could be promoted to *aedile*, who supervised commerce, food supplies, public works and entertainment.

Becoming a praetor would be the next step. Praetors either acted as provincial governors or judges, managing the law courts.

An ex-praetor could become a consul. Two consuls headed the government, serving for only one year. Many consuls became very rich.

Censors were responsible for drawing up a census of the people, making contracts for public works and collecting taxes.

The Senate was an advisory council of elders. Consuls automatically became senators. The office of senator was lifelong.

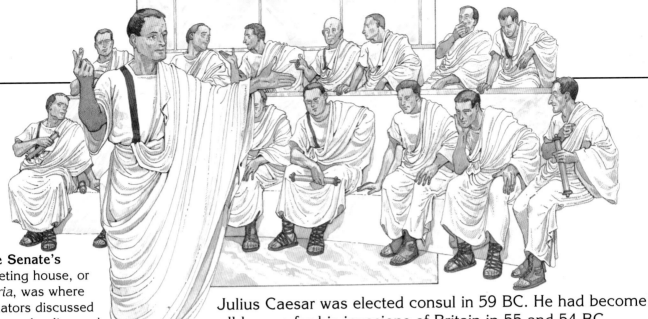

The Senate's meeting house, or *Curia*, was where senators discussed laws and policy and received foreign ambassadors. A Roman senator wore a heavy woollen toga with a broad purple trim.

Julius Caesar was elected consul in 59 BC. He had become well known for his invasions of Britain in 55 and 54 BC, although not all his campaigns were as successful. Caesar fought for power over his rival, Pompey. Caesar won and became dictator, but was murdered by a group of senators in 44 BC. Following his death civil war erupted. Two men struggled for power - Mark Antony and Octavian (Caesar's adopted son). Octavian won, becoming the first emperor of Rome, and in 27 BC he was given the name Augustus. Augustus brought an end to the civil wars, bringing peace and prosperity - the 'pax romana' - back to the provinces. During his forty-year reign as emperor, Augustus reformed every aspect of government, from the army to taxes, coinage and justice. He was the first of a line of emperors that ruled until AD 476, some of them more wisely than others.

Double-headed silver coin, a *denarius* c.AD 140, (left) showing Antoninus Pius and Marcus Aurelius.

This Republican denarius, c.137 BC (below) would have paid a legionary soldier for about three days, and bought enough wheat to bake his daily bread for nearly a month. The reverse side shows Romulus and Remus suckling on the she-wolf.

This Roman coin called a *sestertius* c.AD 196 (above), shows the portrait of the eight-year-old Caracalla, the heir of Septimus Severus. The reverse bears the Latin for 'perpetual security' - a reference to the frontier wars of the time.

ROME, CAPITAL CITY

Rome's power grew rapidly under the Republic. The warlike tribes of the Samnites and the Etruscans were defeated and, secure in Italy, the Romans embarked on a campaign against Carthage in North Africa - the Punic Wars (264 and 146 BC), which won them their first overseas territories: Sicily, Sardinia and Corsica. As the Romans began their conquest of the world with what their enemies called 'rhom' (the Greek word for brute force), profits flowed back into Rome and a new city began to arise. Rome grew haphazardly. As it became more powerful, brick buildings gave way to stone and then to marble. Huge palaces, great temples and vast public squares were built on a scale never seen before. Aqueducts carried water from the mountains into the public fountains, providing all the citizens of Rome with clean water to drink and to bathe in.

The Circus Maximus

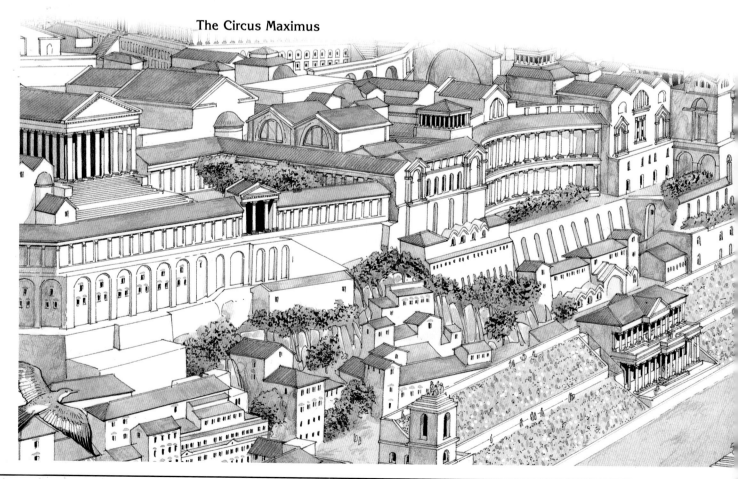

The River Tiber

The River Tiber (above), at 406 km long, is the second longest river in Italy after the Po. The Tiber had been an important river for trade since the Punic Wars when the harbour at Ostia became a key naval base. As the harbour silted up at the end of the first century AD, a new road called the Via Portuense was built to connect Rome with the imperial port of Fimicinio, which had been established a little to the north of Ostia itself.

The Circus Maximus (below) was one of the largest structures ever built by the Romans. Since the foundation of Rome the site had been used for horse racing. But Julius Caesar had the 'spina' (the track) shortened and made into an arena for holding gladiatorial contests.

ALL ROADS LEAD TO ROME

New roads and the use of maps made communications easier. The Roman army built thousands of miles of roads for military use, which were later used by merchants. Milestones along the roadside gave the mileage to the nearest large city. Travelling could be long and arduous. The imperial post could travel at just eight kilometres an hour over long distances, including stopover time. Elegant Romans chose the Via Appia, one of the main roads in and out of Rome, to show off their splendid vehicles. Carriages could be hired outside the city gates, with relay stations along the route to provide fresh mules or horses. Carriages carried a number of passengers but, because they had no springs, travelling could be slow and uncomfortable. Terrible punishments were inflicted on highwaymen if they were caught, nevertheless most travellers remained in a constant state of fear of being robbed. It was slightly safer to travel in the company of high officials.

Groma

Building a road

Soldiers dug a deep ditch on each side of the line of the road and threw earth towards the centre.

No burials could take place within the city walls. In the 2nd century AD a law was passed that bodies had to be buried beyond the city limits, in order to prevent the spread of disease.

Mosaic from Ostia (left) showing a cart being pulled by two mules.

The Via Appia named after the censor Appius Claudius Caecus, was the first link in a network of roads that eventually covered over 96,500 km. The Via Appia connected Rome to the main towns and ports in the south of Italy, and parts of it still stand today.

Tomb-lined roads existed outside most towns and cities.

THE FORUM ROMANUM

Most Roman towns or cities had a forum, similar to a town square today around which stood public buildings like the basilica or hall of justice, where all public meetings were held. As the Forum Romanum (Roman Forum) gradually lost its original purpose as a centre for politics and commerce, it became a sacred area symbolising the might of Rome, and commemorating past victories and events. Roman emperors erected magnificent public buildings around the Forum. Augustus justifiably boasted that: 'I left Rome a city of marble, though I found it a city of brick' (although he was probably thinking of the public squares rather than the squalid slums). Augustus wanted to make Rome a city worthy of governing an empire. He spent vast sums of his own money on new buildings, employing the best architects and sculptors of the day. The city was further transformed by a later building program by Emperor Nero, following the Great Fire of AD 64 that had devastated Rome; only four of its 14 regions escaped the blaze.

Remains of the Forum Romanum looking towards the Colosseum. The first great builder was Julius Caesar, followed by Caesar Augustus. The marshy land was drained and levelled off, and existing buildings were embellished and enlarged.

1 Tabularium. 2 Portico of Dii Consentes (Porch of the gods). Gilded bronze statues of the gods were placed here to be worshipped. 3 Temple of Vespasian and Temple of Concordia, erected in honour of two emperors. 4 Temple of Saturn. 5 Basilica of Julia. 6 Temple of the Dioscuri. 7 Palace of Tiberius and Temple of Augustus. 8 Temple of Vesta where the sacred flame perpetually burned. The temple repeatedly burnt down until it was rebuilt in brick. If the flame went out it was a sign that Rome would be plagued by bad luck. 9 House of the Vestals. 10 Arch of Titus. 11 Temple of Venus and Roma. 12 Basilica of Maxentius. 13 Temples of Antoninus and Faustina. 14 Basilica Emilia, built after Rome's victory over Carthage. 15 Curia Julia (The Senate Assembly Hall). About 300 people could be seated in this building. It was built to replace the Curia Hostilia, which burnt down in 52 BC. 16 Arch of Septimius Severus. 17 Mamertine Prison.

VICTORY PROCESSION

The Roman Empire depended on a strong and efficient army. Soldiers were sent to every corner of the Empire to defend its frontiers and put down rebellions. Most soldiers at the time of the empire were volunteers. A Roman citizen could join the army as a legionary; non-citizens joined up as auxiliaries. In wartime a soldier's life was a mixture of long marches, bloody battles and looting. In peacetime soldiers had to construct camps and bridges, and build and repair roads. Triumphal arches had no practical function, but were built to commemorate great campaigns abroad and to celebrate victory in battle. A victorious army, led by its general in his chariot, would march in procession through the streets of Rome, displaying the prisoners it had captured and the treasures it had won on campaign to the cheering crowds.

The Arch of Constantine (above) was built to commemorate Constantine's victory over Maxentius at the Battle of Milvian Bridge in AD 312. It stands to the west of the Colosseum in Rome and panels show the battle as well as Constantine giving gifts to the people of Rome. Many of the carvings were taken from other structures and where another Emperor was featured, his face was re-carved to look like Constantine.

GODS AND TEMPLES

The Ancient Romans believed in life after death. They worshipped many different gods and goddesses, some of whom were based on Greek gods. Roman temples were dedicated to the gods or to the emperor, who was often revered as a god. Temple priests performed sacrifices and conducted religious ceremonies to win the gods' favour. No services were held in the temples, instead people took offerings to please the gods. Romans also prayed daily at small shrines in their homes. People in the provinces worshipped local gods alongside the official Roman gods. Foreign gods were also worshipped in Rome. Mithraism was a foreign religion based around the Persian god Mithras, which was very popular with soldiers. It was a religion for men only, but its followers came from all social classes.

An ox being led to the altar for sacrifice.

Pigs, oxen and many other animals were sacrificed on an altar outside the temple to please the gods. Only a priest called a *harsupex* could perform this ritual.

Symbols of good and evil

Owls may signal disaster.

The sound of bells was thought to ease the pain of childbirth.

Bees were sacred messengers of the gods and symbols of good luck.

Peonies were said to have magical healing powers.

Eagles were said to bring thunderstorms.

Vesta was the Roman goddess of the hearth and household. Her shrine in the Roman Forum was served by six women called Vestal Virgins, who took their vows between the ages of six and ten years of age. Their task was to keep the shrine's sacred fire alight. The Vestal Virgins could not marry, and had to serve for 30 years. If they were disobedient and broke their vows, they were punished by being buried alive; it was forbidden to spill the blood of a Vestal Virgin.

Christianity was one of the foreign religions introduced into Rome. From a small group of followers of Jesus of Nazareth, over the course of around 300 years Christianity grew to become the official religion of the Roman Empire. The early Christians were attacked by Jewish leaders called the *Pharisees*, and driven from Judaea into Syria. The Christian faith spread under the leadership of Jesus's disciples Peter, Paul and Simon.

Religious festivals were held every month in honour of particular gods. Many of these were public holidays with games and celebrations. The Saturnalia was held in December to mark the end of the planting season. Slaves were granted some freedom during this festival and, in a reversal of roles, were waited on by their masters! People crowned a mock king and gave presents to one another.

The Pantheon in Rome is one of the greatest surviving masterpieces of Roman architecture. Begun by Agrippa in 27 BC, but rebuilt by Hadrian between AD 118 and 125, it was built to honour all of the gods. The vast dome of the Pantheon (43 m in diameter) was covered with gilded bronze and could be seen gleaming from all over Rome. The only light for the interior comes through an opening at the very apex of the dome.

ROMAN GODS

Jupiter, king of the gods

Juno, Jupiter's wife

Minerva, goddess of wisdom

Diana, goddess of hunting

Venus, goddess of love

Isis, an Egyptian goddess

Mithras, a Persian god

Bacchus, god of wine

Pan, god of mountains, flocks and herds

A RICH MAN'S HOUSE

The 14 regions of Rome were divided into areas called *vici*. These were run by officers called *aediles*. In the vici people of extreme poverty and extreme wealth lived side by side. However, a rich family would live in a mansion called a *domus*, where the noise and the dangers of the city were removed. This domus had certain features: an *atrium* (main hall) with an opening in the roof to catch rainwater, a *triclinium* (formal dining room), and one or more enclosed courtyards with beautiful gardens. In some of the most luxurious houses water spouts gushed into marble-lined pools. Skilled artists decorated these great houses by painting beautiful frescoes on the walls and creating complex mosaic floors. A means of central heating called *hypocaust* kept the cold at bay. Furniture was made from expensive and rare woods, which were inlaid with bronze and ivory.

The *triclinium* or dining room was a small room furnished with three or four couches and a few small tables. Slaves would wait on diners here.

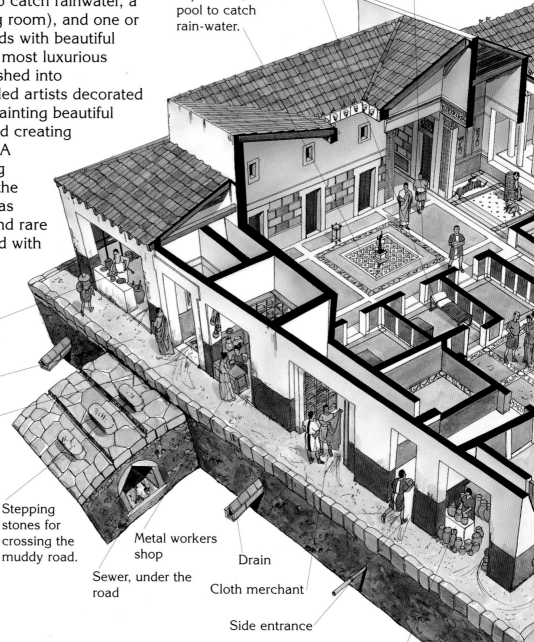

Walls, showing brick patterns.

The *atrium* or main hall, could be used as a living room.

Impluvium, a small pool to catch rain-water.

Thermopolium (cooked food shop)

Shops. The shopkeepers paid rent to the owner of the domus.

Main entrance

Stepping stones for crossing the muddy road.

Metal workers shop

Sewer, under the road

Drain

Cloth merchant

Side entrance

Olive oil merchant

Many slaves would work in a house like this: cooks, maids, cleaners, gardeners and companions. A slave might work as a teacher for the younger boys of the household.

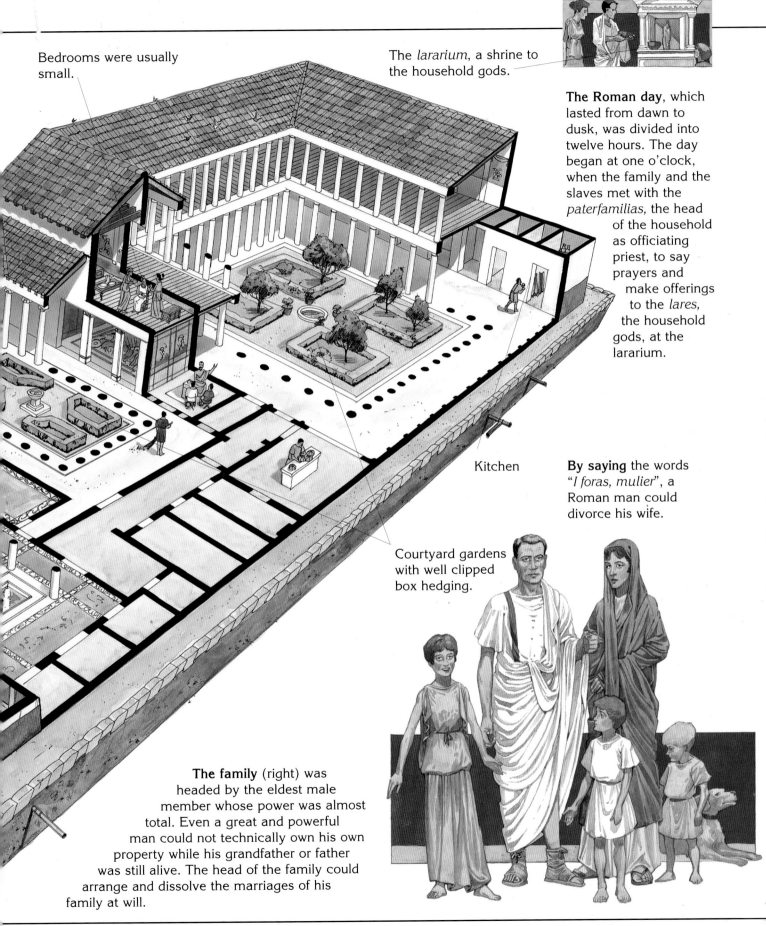

Bedrooms were usually small.

The *lararium*, a shrine to the household gods.

The Roman day, which lasted from dawn to dusk, was divided into twelve hours. The day began at one o'clock, when the family and the slaves met with the *paterfamilias,* the head of the household as officiating priest, to say prayers and make offerings to the *lares,* the household gods, at the lararium.

Kitchen

By saying the words "*I foras, mulier*", a Roman man could divorce his wife.

Courtyard gardens with well clipped box hedging.

The family (right) was headed by the eldest male member whose power was almost total. Even a great and powerful man could not technically own his own property while his grandfather or father was still alive. The head of the family could arrange and dissolve the marriages of his family at will.

THE PUBLIC BATHS

Bathing is an essential part of hygiene throughout the world, particularly in warm climates. The Romans took enormous pleasure in the rituals of the public baths, and not simply to keep clean. They came to exercise, to meet with friends, to have massages or beauty treatments, to relax and gossip, and even to do business. Both public and private baths were laid out in the same way, only their size differed. Some public baths were so large that an Ancient Roman named Ammianus Marcellinus compared them to the provinces! The Baths of Caracalla in Rome covered 13 hectares. It had a stadium and space for 1600 bathers. As the admission fee was inexpensive, a wide range of people went to the baths. Accompanied by their slaves, the very wealthy enjoyed its pleasures alongside the very poor. Unattended clothes were often stolen.

Public toilet

Toilets with running water were rarely found in private houses. Communal toilets were used. A wet sponge stick was shared by all and used instead of toilet paper.

Reconstruction of a sponge stick.

The Baths of Caracalla, built in AD 212-217 by the Emperor Caracalla.

Channel for water

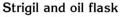

Aqueducts (below) brought fresh water to Rome. One of the most important aqueducts was the *Aqua Claudia,* begun in AD 38 by Caligula and completed by Claudius in AD 52. It brought water to the city from a source near Subiaco 68 km away.

Strigil and oil flask (below) The Romans did not have soap, instead they rubbed oil on their bodies and scraped off the sweat, dirt and oil with an instrument called a *strigil*. At the baths men had their unwanted body hair plucked by slaves with tweezers called *alipili*. This was an expensive and painful procedure.

GOING TO THE BATHS

Leave clothes in the *apodyterium* (the changing room). A *capsarius* (attendant) can be paid to make sure they are not stolen.

Exercise. Some people choose to lift lead weights or run round the baths.

Tepidarium. A warm room for bathers with a small pool and a larger one for swimming. Ideal for relaxing and gossiping.

Caldarium. A very hot room to make you sweat. The temperature could be stifling.

Frigidarium. A very cold pool to plunge into after the heat of the *caldarium*.

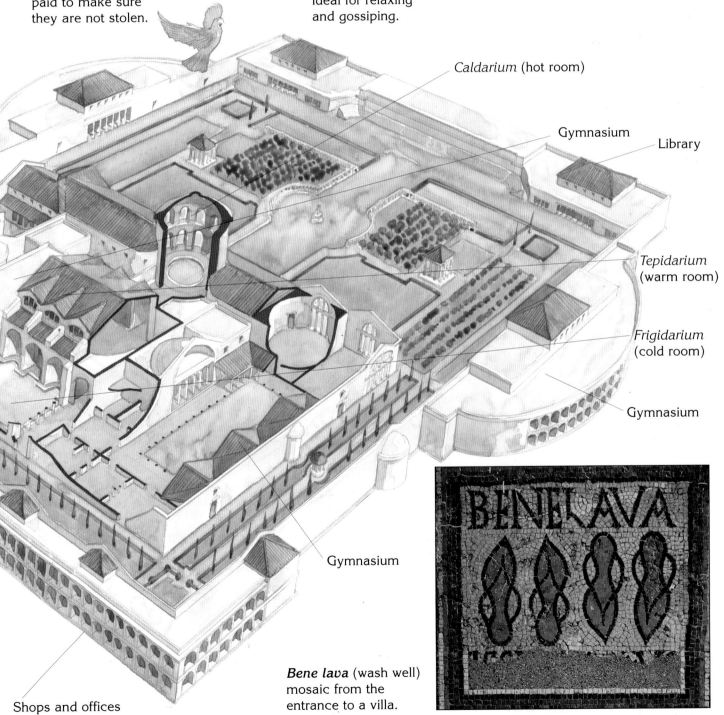

Caldarium (hot room)

Gymnasium

Library

Tepidarium (warm room)

Frigidarium (cold room)

Gymnasium

Gymnasium

Shops and offices

Bene lava (wash well) mosaic from the entrance to a villa.

SHOPS AND WORK

Sandal maker

Potter

Most of the streets in Rome were lined with shops and workshops, which opened early each morning and closed at dusk, with a short break at mid-day. Money was used everywhere for buying and selling goods and for paying taxes. Outside every public building, including the baths, the theatre and the circus, there were merchants selling wine and cooked foods. They displayed their goods in front of a stall, beneath a painted board intended to attract customers. Some merchants also did business wandering the streets, selling small items like sulphur matches in exchange for bits of broken glass. Every nine days markets called the *nundines* were held, where people came from the country to sell their produce and buy whatever they needed to take back home. The markets of the Saepta Julia were visited by many people, who came to see the works of art and luxury objects sold there.

A great variety of craftsmen were needed to keep the city supplied with goods. There were smiths, potters, sculptors, glass blowers, carpenters, masons and bone carvers. Fathers passed their skills on to their sons, so whole families would work together.

Carpenters (above) made furniture or worked on wooden buildings.

Cloth cleaners (below) called 'fullers' also prepared new cloth.

Cloth soaked in urine (collected in the streets).

Stiffened cloth is washed with 'fullers earth'.

The cloth is beaten and stretched to flatten it.

Rinsed, dried over frames and then pressed.

A Roman butcher (above) 2nd century AD, from a relief excavated at Ostia.

A knife seller

Goods were often produced at the back of the shop. Other goods arrived by cart during the night. Traders used a weighing scale called a 'steel yard', which worked by hanging goods from hooks and moving a weight along the scale until it balanced.

Imperial Rome was a huge city with a population of over a million people, most of whom lived in small rooms over shops or in squalid slums. Blocks of flats called *insulae* (the Latin word for 'island') were crammed together in dark narrow streets. Here poor families would live in wretched, cramped conditions. The insulae were built ever higher in order to cram in more and more people, until laws were eventually passed limiting them to a height of four or five storeys. However, landlords tended to ignore these laws and, as a result, insulae often collapsed. One wealthy landlord named Cicero complained that: "Two of my buildings have collapsed, and in the others the walls have all cracked. Not only have the tenants, but even the mice have left." The upper storeys, which were usually built of wood, were fire hazards, as the tenants used charcoal braziers for cooking and heating. Sparks from these could easily set material or wooden furniture alight.

A poor man started his day very early when the sun rose.

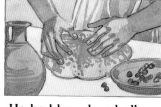

He had bread and olives for breakfast. The very poor received free bread.

His wife collected water from the public fountain.

He worked on a hot food stall.

He had to have dinner before it got dark – there was no money to spare for lamp oil.

He went to bed as soon as it got dark.

The remains of an apartment block at Ostia, near Rome (above). The arched doorways on the ground floor were the entrances to shops and taverns. Stairs led up to the flats above.

Slaves were at the bottom of the social pyramid. The settled order of Roman life was dependent on its slave workforce. Slaves had no rights and could be bought and sold. During the period of the republic, slaves were totally under the control of their masters. In the imperial period slaves were treated slightly better: they were protected from savage masters and, more importantly, they could look forward to eventual *manumission*, or freedom.

THE CIRCUS FLAVIUS

The Circus Flavius, Rome's oval amphitheatre, is now known as the Colosseum. It was the scene of brutal gladiatorial games. Emperor Vespasian started the construction of the Colosseum in AD 72. As the site had formerly been a lake in the gardens of Emperor Nero's Golden House, it had to be drained first and kept dry. Built of concrete and marble, the Colosseum took eight years to complete, and was finally opened by Vespasian's son, the Emperor Titus. It had the capacity to hold around 55,000 people, and had 80 separate entrances called *vomitoria*, which were designed so that the entire venue could be filled or emptied in less than 15 minutes.

Gladiators were professional fighters, usually prisoners, slaves or criminals, who were trained in different ways of fighting at gladiatorial schools. Impresarios were always looking for new types of contests. Unequal matches were popular; for example, a gladiator might be forced to fight a lion that had been brought to the edge of madness through starvation.

The first recorded gladiatorial games were held in 264 BC as part of the funeral of a nobleman. Emperor Trajan held the biggest games at the Colosseum in AD 107: more than 10,000 gladiators fought and 11,000 animals died.

Gladiatorial helmet from Pompeii. Gladiator armour was designed more for spectacular theatrical effect rather than to protect its wearer.

The poet Juvenal said that the Roman people were only interested in bread and circuses. The emperors provided them with free food in the form of grain and meat (*dole*), and entertainments like chariot racing, wild beast fights and gladiatorial contests. One of the chief purposes of these spectacles was to provide a diversion for the hordes of unemployed Romans, who could number as many as 150,000.

Under the Colosseum (above) a network of tunnels, chambers and prisons were used to house the scenery, animals, gladiators and prisoners. There was also a pit for the dead bodies, which were hauled off the arena by a man dressed as the god Mercury, and armed with ropes and metal hooks. (Mercury escorted souls to the Underworld).

The ruins of the Colosseum (below) still stand in the centre of Rome.

The Circus games were finally banned in AD 404.

The Colosseum was supported by many arched concrete vaults. People were issued with numbered tickets and entered through one of the 80 entrances.

ROMAN CLOTHES

From the earliest times right up until the imperial period Roman men wore the same garment every day: a toga. Only citizens were allowed to wear a toga. Many people found it too heavy and cumbersome in the summer, preferring to wear a simple tunic for work and sleep. Emperor Augustus's decree that togas must be worn at any public assembly was often ignored. Home-produced clothing was generally worn. Spinning and weaving was done at home by free women and slaves. Augustus kept his family very busy by making a point of wearing home-spun cloth; in his household 18 slaves were employed to make and repair clothes. Silk, linen and other fine textiles were also imported from Asia and Egypt. As these fabrics were expensive, they were only worn by extremely wealthy Romans.

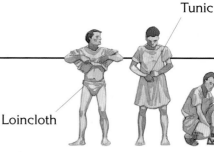

A poor man wears a simple tunic, with a loincloth underneath.

The tunic is belted. He wears a woollen cloak and sandals.

One end of the toga is draped over the left shoulder.

The other end goes under the right arm and over the left shoulder.

Women's clothing, like men's, did not change its basic shape much over the years. Fabrics and accessories changed, but the tunic remained the same.

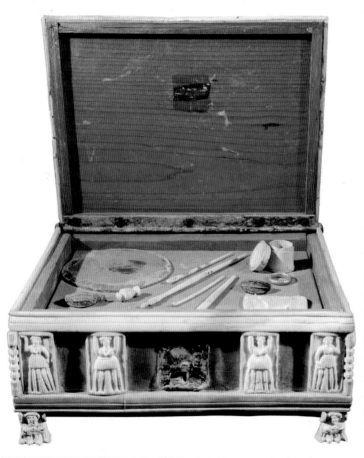

Toilet casket (left) from Campania in Italy. Wealthy Roman women had many cosmetic aids. Bear fat was used to make their hair grow, and a mixture made from ants eggs was used to blacken their eyebrows. Some used a face cream made from crushed sun-dried snails mixed with bean broth!

Children wore miniature versions of adult clothes. The most important day in a Roman boy's life was when he was given his *toga virilis*, which symbolised his new-found rank of man and citizen. He would also abandon all childhood toys at this time. The ceremony was held in March during the feast of the god Bacchus.

Poor people and slaves wore a simple tunic, which had to be constantly patched and mended. The *lacerna* was a hooded cloak, used particularly in winter to provide better protection against wind and rain.

A Roman woman's hair was the most important part of her beauty preparations. Slaves were appointed especially to look after their mistresses hair. If a woman thought her hairdresser had not followed her instructions she could be very spiteful and summon the public torturer.

Gold earring (right), 2nd century BC. The rich preferred gold and silver jewellery. Poor people wore jewellery made from cheaper materials like ceramics and bronze. Wealthy Romans took great pride in owning their own seals, which had to be as individual and artistic as possible. The concentration of great wealth attracted Greek and Oriental craftsmen to the capital.

Palla (cloak)

Stola (robe)

Tunic

Toga

When out walking wealthy women wore a *stola*, a long robe fastened by a brooch, which came down to their heels. They also wrapped themselves in a *palla* or cloak. Most women wore veils that partially obscured their faces. This may have harked back to an ancient custom whereby Roman women were forbidden by law to go out with their faces uncovered.

Calceus, shoes worn in public with the toga.

FOOD

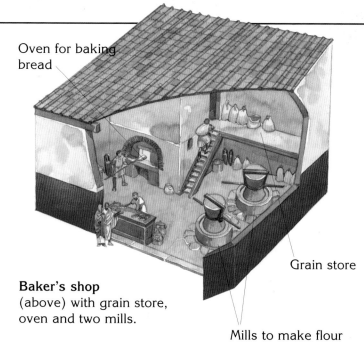

Oven for baking bread

Baker's shop
(above) with grain store, oven and two mills.

Grain store

Mills to make flour

A kitchen was a luxury in an ancient Roman house. Poor people who lived in flats were lucky if they even had a simple brazier to cook on. Many poor Romans had to go out to eat in taverns or bars, or took food to the bakers to be cooked for them. A rich Roman's town house or country villa would have an oven or charcoal stove. Lunch was eaten at about 11 am and was usually a cold meal of bread, salad, olives, cheese, fruit, nuts, and cold meat left over from dinner the night before. Poor people existed mainly on a type of wheat or barley porridge. Although the Roman diet included familiar ingredients like meat, fish and vegetables, they were combined in a way that we might consider odd today. Some food, although common, never became a regular part of the Roman diet. Butter was used only as a medicine and milk as a cosmetic. Wealthy Romans held elaborate dinner parties. A formal dinner usually had nine guests, who reclined on couches set out in a U shape around the table. Slaves would wait on the guests and entertain them with music and singing.

Thermopolium
(a hot food shop)

Amphorae, pottery jars containing wine and food, were sunk into the marble counter. Few people had cooking facilities so they had to buy prepared food from hot food shops.

Saucepan, 1st century AD

A RICH FAMILY'S DINNER PARTY

The *triclinium* (dining room) was decorated with fresh flowers.

Guests arrived, bringing their own napkins.

Slaves washed guests' hands and fanned them while they ate.

The *gustus* (first course) of jellyfish and eggs was served.

A slave called a *structor* set out the dishes for each course.

First pluck the flamingo. Wash and place in a pan of lightly salted water.

Only young, good-looking slaves were allowed to serve wine.

A slave called the *scissor* cut the meat into bite-sized pieces.

The *cena* (main course) may have been ostrich, flamingo or dormouse.

Secunda mensa (dessert) was usually fruit or sweet pastries.

The guests left after midnight with their napkins full of leftovers.

Season with dill and a little vinegar. Bring to the boil and simmer until the meat is tender.

Thicken the cooking liquid with flour to make a sauce.

Flavour the sauce with mixed spices. Finally, add the dates to the sauce. The same recipe can be used for cooking parrot.

The Roman diners feasted lavishly on a selection of exotic novelty dishes. A meal might start with a choice of sows udders with salted sea urchins or a paté of brains cooked with milk and eggs. The main course could be turtle dove boiled in its feathers or dormice rubbed with honey, stuffed with figs and bayleaves and baked in a pastry. Desserts included hot African sweet wine cakes or stoned dates with nuts and pine kernels.

In the triclinium there were usually three couches, each large enough to hold three guests. An ideal party would be between three and nine guests.

ART AND ARCHITECTURE

Many artists, architects, sculptors and craftsmen worked on public and private buildings in Rome. Because of its great wealth, the city attracted the most talented people from all over the Empire. Wealthy senators and merchants bought works of art for their villas, dined off silver plates, and commissioned expensive mosaic floors. Massive public buildings and monuments glorified the emperors and were an outward display of imperial power. The emperors funded some of these building programmes themselves. The ruins of Emperor Hadrian's villa still stand outside Rome today. On his 60 hectare estate, which was 27 km from Rome, he built theatres, libraries and baths. The villa gardens contained copies of famous Greek and Egyptian statues. The Romans borrowed many artistic styles from the Etruscans and the Greeks.

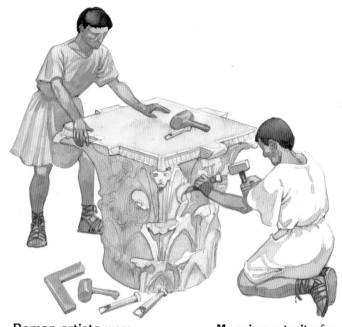

Roman artists were expected to follow their patrons' orders, rather than express their own artistic style.

Mosaic portrait of a woman (right). Mosaic was used to decorate floors and walls. It was made of tiny cubes of glass set into a layer of wet mortar.

The lost wax process

  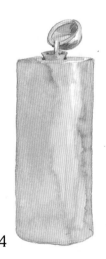 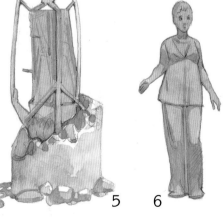

1   2   3   4   5   6

To make a bronze statue, a sculptor uses the 'lost wax' process:
(1) A statue is made out of clay.
(2) The clay statue is covered in wax. Details are now carved into the wax. A further layer of clay is added.
(3) The statue is turned upside down. Tubes are attached so that molten metal can be poured in. Another layer of clay is added.

(4) The statue is fired in an oven. The wax melts and runs off. Molten bronze is now poured in to this gap.
(5) The whole structure must be left to cool. Then the outermost layer of clay (the mould) is broken, revealing the bronze statue.
(6) The sculptor then puts the finishing touches to the statue, carefully polishing it until the bronze shines.

TRADE

An orator in the second century AD said: "All that trade and ships may bring reaches Rome". The city lived off its imports, and its merchants were the wealthiest men in the Empire. Huge cargoes came from the provinces to be unloaded in the harbour of Ostia at the mouth of the River Tiber. Pliny the Younger commented that: "in Rome the merchandise of the whole world comes together". Spain supplied Rome with precious metals, olive oil, wine and liquamen. It also exported strong urine for use in the production and cleaning of cloth.

From Africa came wild animals for the gladiatorial arena as well as purple dye, olive oil and corn; and the thriving civilisation of Greece provided the marble that was used for many of Rome's finest buildings. Most of the corn that fed the Empire came from Egypt along with papyrus, flax and dates. The Eastern provinces supplied silks, spices, dyes and perfumes. Sea crossings were carefully planned. In winter the weather was too bad to sail; in summer there was a risk of being attacked by pirates.

The fine Roman tableware that dates from the early Empire is known as Samian ware. Large-scale production of Samian ware was started in Arretium (modern Arezzo) but around AD 60 Arretium lost its importance as a centre of production when workshops in Gaul became more important. Samian ware was made by pressing clay into moulds made by master craftsmen.

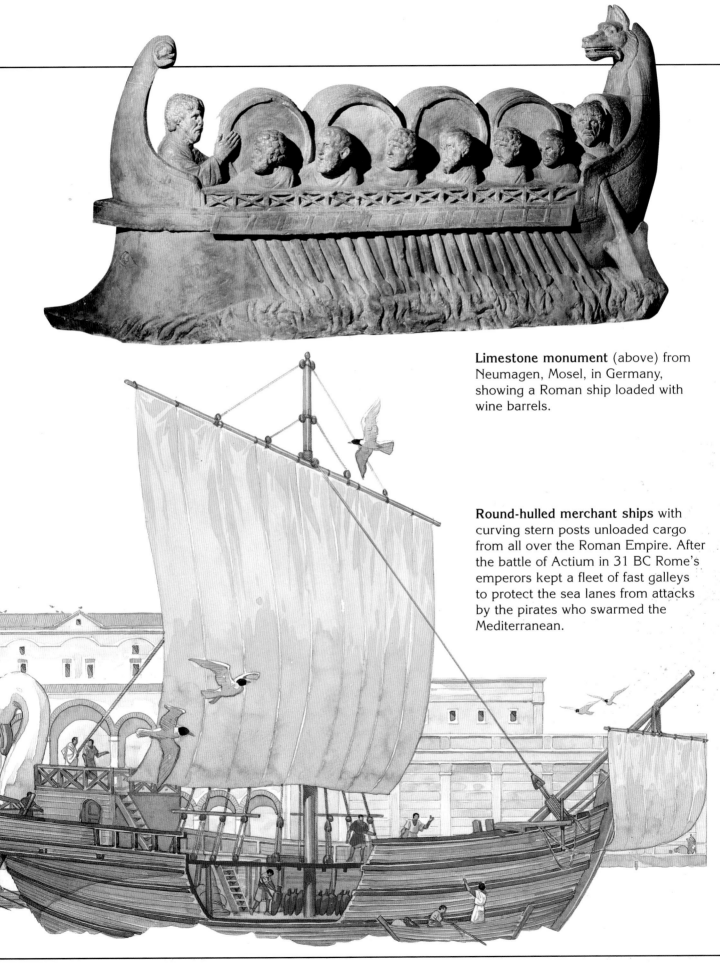

Limestone monument (above) from Neumagen, Mosel, in Germany, showing a Roman ship loaded with wine barrels.

Round-hulled merchant ships with curving stern posts unloaded cargo from all over the Roman Empire. After the battle of Actium in 31 BC Rome's emperors kept a fleet of fast galleys to protect the sea lanes from attacks by the pirates who swarmed the Mediterranean.

DEATH AND FUNERALS

Poor people and slaves were not usually able to afford a funeral; funerals were reserved for the wealthy. Romans who could afford to do so would organise their own funeral arrangements in advance. At best, Romans wished to die at home, surrounded by family. The eldest son would place a coin in the mouth of the deceased. This was to pay the ferryman who the Romans believed took the dead from the land of the living across the River Styx into Hades, the land of the dead. Romans felt that no death was worse than death at sea, as the body had no proper grave. This meant that the soul would not be admitted to the company of the blessed and would wander the shores of the River Styx forever more.

This sarcophagus carved from marble for an extremely wealthy Roman boy (left) shows all the activities he would have enjoyed during his lifetime.

Romans feared dying unmourned. Many people arranged and paid for their funerals well in advance. Professional undertakers embalmed the body before burial or cremation.

Roman carving (right) showing a funeral procession. The body is being carried on a litter to its burial place.

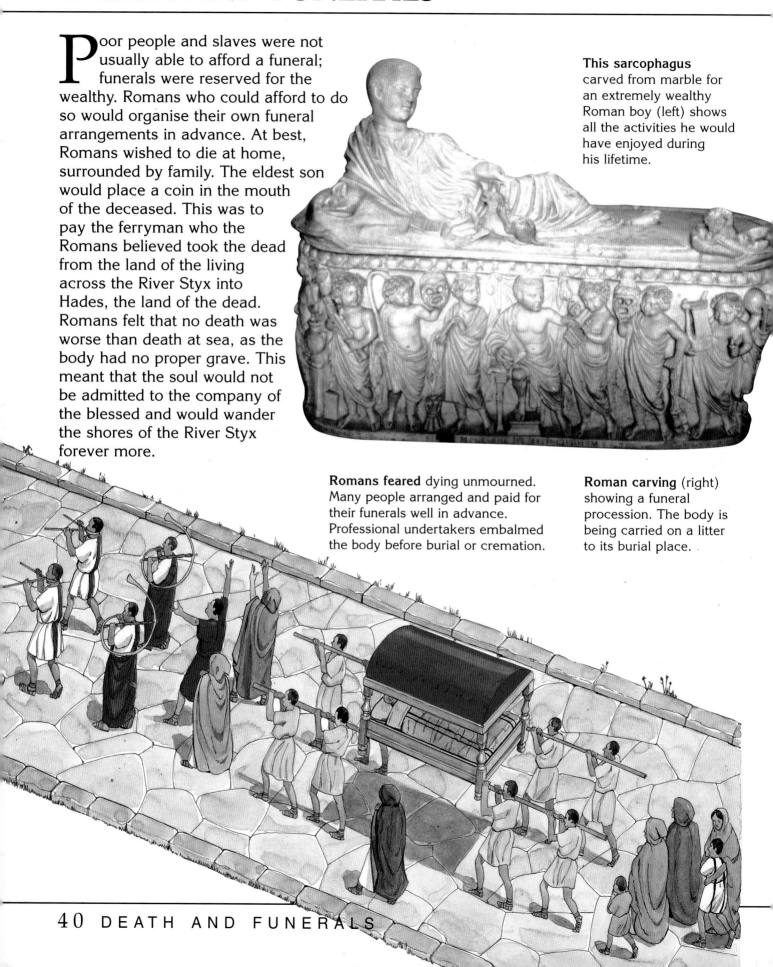

OUTSIDE ROME

Rome was never a healthy city, especially in summer. All those who could afford to do so, fled to the seaside or to the country. To the wealthy Romans, their villa in the country was not just a luxurious house, it included the whole country estate that surrounded it. A large estate was completely self-supporting. The estate farm supplied nearly all the food for its owners and all its farm workers; luxury goods were imported. Skilled craftsmen in the workshops made many of the items needed on the estate. This included clothes, tools, harnesses and farm carts. The estate owner would employ both free men and slaves. In his absence the estate would be run by an estate manager or *vilicus* and his wife, a *vilica*. Many Roman writers were interested in farming, and books on farming advice still survive. They give precise instructions for planning a farm; for example, the kitchens and stables were best situated where they would catch the winter sun, and everything to do with wine-making needed a cool position, while oil-making needed a warm position. The slaves' quarters were located in a part of the estate called the *Villa Rustica*.

The farm buildings were grouped round a small yard.

Kitchen

Oil storage jars

A YEAR ON A GREAT ESTATE

Spring: The land was ploughed by a team of oxen guided by a ploughman. The sheep were sheared; the fleeces washed, spun into thread and woven to make woollen clothing.

Summer: The hay was cut to be stored and fed to the cattle later in the year. The corn was harvested and taken to the granary where it was ground into flour to make bread.

Autumn: The grapes were picked and treaded in a vat to make wine. The juice was strained and stored in jars; the pulp went into the wine press. Autumn was also the lambing season.

Winter: The vines were pruned to make them give good crops the next autumn. Olives were picked. Next year's wheat and barley crops were sown in the spaces between the olive trees.

Olives were a lucrative crop for the villa owner. They were eaten fresh or pickled. They were also grown for their oil, which was used as a body rub at the gym and the baths.

The main part of the villa where the owner would live.

TIMELINE OF ANCIENT ROME

The history of Ancient Rome can be divided into two main periods. The Roman Republic began in about 510 BC and continued until the death of Julius Caesar in 44 BC, which was followed by power struggles and civil war. In 27 BC, the first Roman Emperor, Augustus, seized power and the period known as the Roman Empire began. The date traditionally given for the founding of Rome is 753 BC. The city grew from a group of villages founded on the seven hills beside the River Tiber by tribal people who had migrated into Italy from central Europe over a thousand years before. Legend has it that the first king of Rome was Romulus, one of twin brothers found and raised by a she-wolf. Six other kings succeeded Romulus. In about 510 BC the last of the kings, Tarquinius Superbus (Tarquin the Proud) was driven out of the city and Rome became a republic.

510 BC-27 BC The Roman Republic
Rome gradually emerges as the dominant power in the region. In 390 BC Rome is invaded and plundered by the Gauls (from France). It slowly recovers; the city is rebuilt and reinforced, and the army strengthened. By 285 BC Rome has fought against and beaten the Gauls, Samnites and Etruscans. By 264 BC Rome controls the whole of Italy.

The Punic Wars (264-241 BC, 218-201 BC and 149-146 BC) The major threat to the expansion of Rome in the Mediterranean are the Carthagians from North Africa. The Romans and Carthagians fight three wars, called the Punic Wars. In the last one the Romans defeat Hannibal, the Carthagian leader, and destroy the city of Cathage, which becomes a Roman province. By 31 BC, most of the countries that border the Mediterranean have fallen under Rome's power.

58-44 BC Julius Caesar conquers Gaul and becomes Rome's greatest ruler yet. A group of senators, led by Brutus and Cassius, resent Caesar's power and, on 15 March 44 BC, they murder him in the Senate.

44-27 BC Civil war between forces led by Mark Antony and Octavian, who Julius Caesar had appointed as his heir.

27 BC-AD 14 The Roman Empire is established. Julius Caesar's adopted son, Octavian, defeats his rival, Mark Antony, and his lover, the Egyptian Queen Cleopatra, and becomes the first Emperor of Rome. He takes the name Augustus, which means 'revered one'. From now until his death in AD 14, peace reigns in Rome, and the Roman Empire overseas is expanded.

AD 14-53 The Roman Empire continues to grow, largely due to the work of Augustus in developing an efficient civil service and strong government in the provinces.

AD 54-68 The reign of Emperor Nero during which the Great Fire of AD 64 destroys two-thirds of Rome. The Emperor is supposed to have played his lyre and watched as the city went up in flames.

AD 69-96 The reigns of Emperors Vespasian, Titus and Domitian are known as the Flavian Dynasty. Vespasian orders the building of the Colosseum.

AD 98-117 Reign of Emperor Trajan. The Empire reaches its greatest extent with the conquest of Dacia (Romania) and parts of the Middle East.

AD 117-138 Reign of Emperor Hadrian, Trajan's successor. Hadrian gives up some of the new provinces, believing the Empire is becoming too big and unwieldy. He concentrates on fortifying the borders. Hadrian's Wall is one of the fortifications.

AD 138-180 This work is continued by the next two Emperors, Antoninus Pius and Marcus Aurelius.

AD 193-211 Emperor Septimius Severus establishes firm control after a period of unrest and civil war.

AD 235-268 Reign of Emperor Diocletian after another period of chaos, civil war and invasion. He splits the Empire into two - the Western Empire and the Eastern Empire.

AD 312-337 Emperor Constantine founds the city of Constantinople (modern Istanbul). It becomes the capital of the Eastern Empire, which later becomes known as the Byzantine Empire. Christianity has spread throughout the Roman Empire by this time, but Christians risk persecution. In AD 313 Constantine announces that Christianity is to be tolerated. In AD 380 it becomes the official religion of the Empire under Theodosius I.

AD 400-476 The Western Empire is overrun by barbarian tribes and collapses. Rome is invaded and destroyed; the last Western Emperor, Romulus Augustulus, is deposed.

AD 527-565 Justinian, ruler of the Eastern Empire, regains much of Rome's lost territory but, within a century or so, loses control of most of it. The Eastern Empire is weakened by the spread of Islam but survives until AD 1453 when Constantinople is conquered by the Muslim leader of Turkey, Sultan Mehmet II.

GLOSSARY

aedile a junior government official in charge of public works.

amphitheatre an oval building with a central arena and tiers of seats, designed for the staging of gladiatorial contests.

amphora a pottery container used for storing liquids (plural amphorae).

aqueduct a stone structure to carry fresh water from the hills into a town.

atrium the main room of a Roman house, characterised by an inward-sloping roof with a square central opening and a pool in the floor, an *impluvium*, to collect rainwater.

auxiliaries soldiers recruited from nations outside the Roman Empire.

barbarian people considered by those of another nation or group to have a primitive civilisation.

basilica a large public building, used as a meeting place for merchants, and as the town hall and law court.

brazier a portable container in which a fire is burned. The Romans burned charcoal in their braziers.

cena the main meal of the day, eaten in the late afternoon. Also used to mean the main course.

censor a junior government official in charge of land-ownership.

circus the arena in which chariot races took place.

citizen a Roman who had the right to vote.

consul one of two men who headed the government for a one year term, managing the senate's affairs and commanding the army.

Curia the building where the town council met to discuss government affairs.

dole a government hand-out of meat and bread distributed to the poor.

domus a private town house.

flax a fine textile fibre used to make thread, which could be woven into linen fabric.

forum a large open area in the centre of Roman towns, where important public meetings were held. It was also a marketplace.

fresco a wall painting in which the paint is applied when the plaster is still wet.

fuller a person who cleaned clothes and prepared cloth for making into clothes.

fuller's earth an absorbent clay-like soil used to shrink and thicken woollen cloth.

galley a warship powered by oars, usually rowed by slaves.

groma an instrument used by a surveyor or architect for measuring straight lines.

impresario a sponsor who books and stages public entertainments.

insula a block of flats or group of buildings.

lararium a small shrine to the 'lares', the guardian spirits of the household, found in every Roman home.

liquamen a popular, strong-tasting sauce made from fermented fish, probably used to hide the taste of food that was not very fresh.

manumission the freedom granted to or bought by slaves.

molten reduced to liquid through heating.

mortar a mixture of cement or lime, sand and water that hardens in place and is used to bind together bricks and stones.

mosaic a decorative surface for floors and walls, made by setting tiny cubes of coloured stone or glass into a base of freshly applied mortar.

orator a skilled public speaker.

papyrus an early form of paper made from the fibre of the papyrus plant.

paterfamilias the head of a household; the father of the family.

patrician a top-ranking nobleman.

plebs (or **plebians**) the ordinary people of Rome.

praetor a judge in the Roman lawcourts or a provincial governor.

province an area outside Rome that was under Roman control.

Punic Wars a series of wars fought between Rome and the city of Carthage.

quaestor a junior government official in charge of finance and administration.

relief a sculpture carved so that shapes on the surface stand out from the background.

republic a country that is not ruled by a king or emperor but is governed by a group of officials elected by the people.

Saepta Julia formerly a building used for the elections, it was later turned into a big bazaar.

sarcophagus a stone coffin, usually inscribed or decorated with sculptures.

senator a member of the Senate, the ruling council of Rome.

tepidarium the room at the baths which was kept at moderate temperature, for massage and resting. The hot room was called the *caldarium*, and the cold room the *frigidarium*.

thermopolium a shop where poorer Romans could buy hot meals.

toga a garment worn by men and boys.

tribune an officer elected by the people to protect their rights.

tributum a direct tax that was levied at times of war.

INDEX